This library edition published in 2011 by Walter Foster Publishing, Inc.
Walter Foster Library
Distributed by Black Rabbit Books.
P.O. Box 3263 Mankato, Minnesota 56002

Printed in China by PRINTPLUS Limited, Shenzhen.

First Library Edition

Library of Congress Cataloging-in-Publication Data

Farrell, Russell.
  Learn to draw sea creatures : learn to draw and color 25 favorite ocean animals, step by easy step, shape by simple shape! / illustrated by Russell Farrell. – 1st library ed.
      p. cm.
  ISBN 978-1-936309-19-1 (hardcover)
  1. Marine animals in art–Juvenile literature. 2. Drawing–Technique–Juvenile literature. I. Title. II. Title: Learn to draw and color 25 favorite ocean animals, step by easy step, shape by simple shape!
  NC781.F37 2011
  743.6–dc22

                                                                              2010004206

022010
OP1825

9 8 7 6 5 4 3 2 1

Learn to Draw

Sea Creatures

Learn to draw and color 25 favorite
ocean animals, step by easy step,
shape by simple shape!

Illustrated by Russell Farrell

Getting Started

When you **look** closely at the **drawings** in this book, you'll notice that they're made up of basic shapes, such as circles, triangles, and rectangles. To draw all your underwater favorites, just start with simple shapes as you see here. It's easy and fun!

Circles are used to draw eyes, heads, and round bodies.

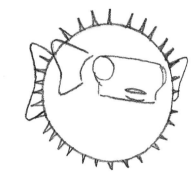

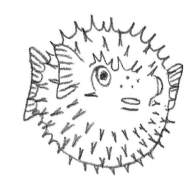

Ovals are good for drawing sea creature profiles.

Triangles are best for drawing the heads of some fish.

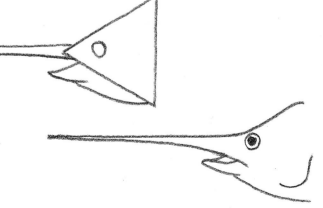

Coloring Tips

There's more than one way to bring your **ocean friends** to life on paper—you can use crayons, markers, or colored pencils. Just be sure you have plenty of good seaworthy colors—blue, green, and purple, plus yellow and orange.

Pencil

Colored pencil

Crayon

Marker

Puffer

The body of the **puffer** is one of the **simplest** shapes of all sea creatures—its body is nearly a perfect circle!

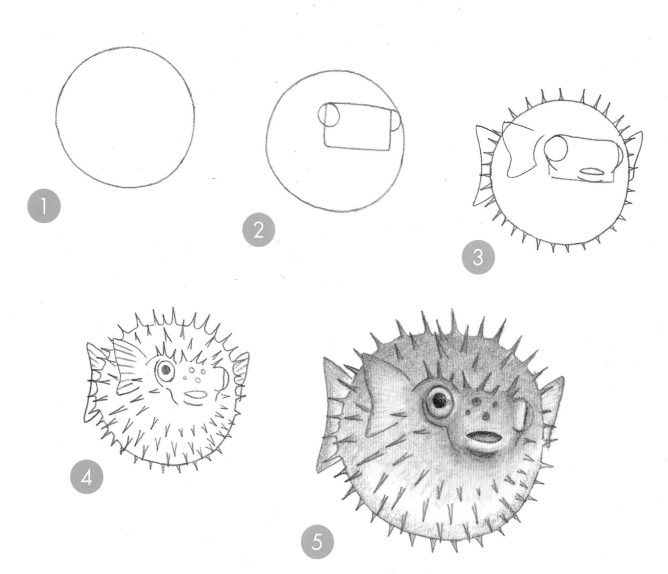

① ② ③ ④ ⑤

fun fact

With all the predators in the ocean, many fish have adapted unique ways to defend themselves. The puffer (also called the "blowfish" or "swellfish") can fill itself up with air or water to become a round, spiky ball, making it very difficult to swallow!

Angelfish

An **elegant** creature, this **tropical** fish is known for its vibrant stripes of color.

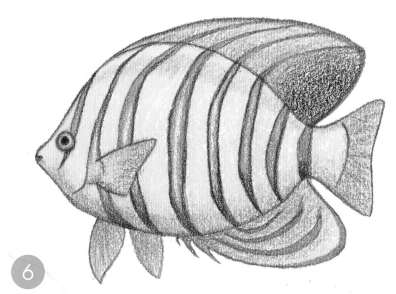

Harp Seal

Draw this **sweet** baby harp seal with **rounded**, gently curving lines and big, dark, "puppy-dog" eyes.

fun fact — A baby harp seal is born with thick white fur, but after 1-1/2 weeks it develops a gray-brown coat with darker, harp-shaped (or horseshoelike) patches.

Sea Star

Start drawing this **sea** animal with simple **circles!**
Then add five triangular arms to create the star shape.

1

2

3

4

5

Humpback Whale

Weighing in at **2 tons,** the humpback is a **whale** of a creature—its huge fins are nearly 1/3 as long as its body!

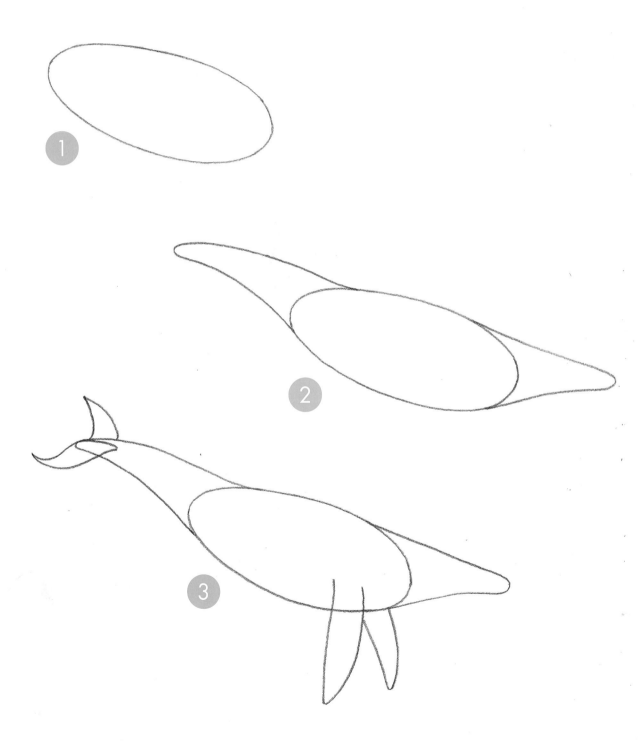

fun fact

This 40-foot creature has a unique way of hunting: It swims in circles around schools of fish while releasing air, creating a curtain of bubbles that traps the fish.

Sea Otter

This **cute** critter has **webbed** back feet, tiny ears, a foot-long tail, and thick brown fur.

Sunfish

Also called a **"moonfish"** because of its round, **white** body, this unique creature has two huge fins and a "barely there" tail.

1
2
3
4
5

Pilot Whale

The **majestic** pilot whale has a distinct **rounded** head, a small beak, and a long, stocky body.

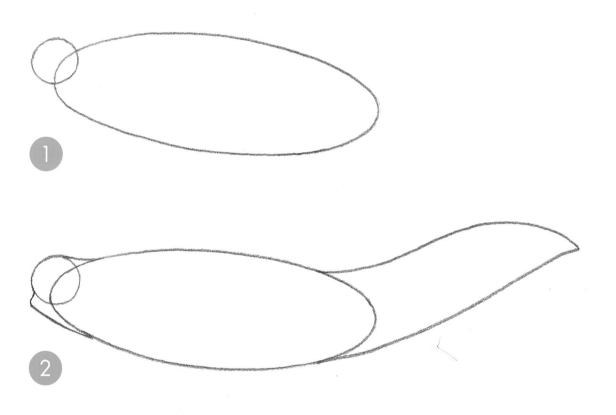

1

2

fun fact

These social sea creatures travel in herds of up to 200, so it's no wonder that pilot whales have developed a complex system for communicating by sounds. With a wide range of whistles, squeaks, and clicks, they are some of the noisiest animals in the ocean!

Clownfish

A **popular saltwater** aquarium creature, the eye-catching clownfish sports bright gold bands of color.

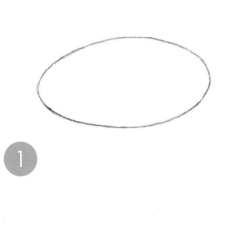

1

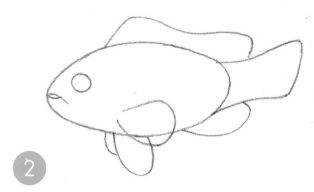

2

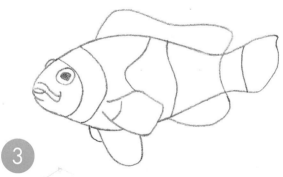

3

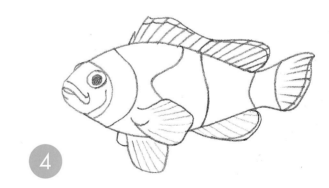

4

fun fact

The clownfish and sea anemone (an animal on the seafloor that resembles a flower) depend on one another for survival. After the anemone catches and eats a fish, the clownfish gets the leftovers that float nearby. In return, the clownfish protects the anemone from predators.

5

Stingray

A **bottom-dweller,** the stingray has a thin, **flat** body that allows it to both hide in the sand and glide through the water.

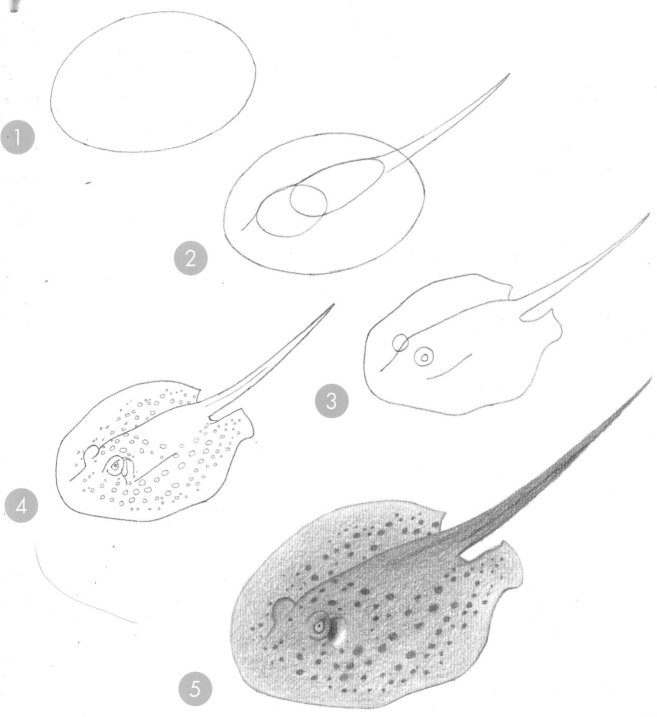

Great White Shark

The most **feared** of all sharks, this **predator** has a long, pointed snout and razor-sharp, triangular teeth.

OCEAN BASICS
There are four major oceans on Earth. From largest to smallest, they are the Pacific Ocean, the Atlantic Ocean, the Indian Ocean, and the Arctic Ocean.

1

2

3

fun fact

Incredibly, a great white has about 3,000 jagged teeth, which are arranged in several rows. The shark uses only the first two rows for capturing prey; the rest of the teeth move into position when the front teeth are damaged or fall out.

Dolphin

A **playful,** intelligent animal, the **dolphin** has a bottle-shaped beak and a happy expression that shows its friendly nature.

1

2

OCEAN BASICS

As the world's second fastest growing plant, kelp (or seaweed) grows up to 2 feet per day. And most people don't know that this super plant is used in a lot of everyday products, including lipstick, ketchup, and ice cream!

3

4

5

fun fact

If you ever see a one-eyed dolphin underwater, chances are it's just sleeping! Because a dolphin can stay underwater for only 10 minutes before returning to the surface for air, it has to remain somewhat awake at all times. As a result, only one-half of the brain—and one eye—sleeps at one time!

Underwater World

After you've learned to **draw** all the **fascinating** creatures in this book, try creating an awesome underwater scene!

Eel

With its single **fin** and **slithery**, snakelike shape, this creature is hard to mistake! Use long, S-shaped lines to draw the eel.

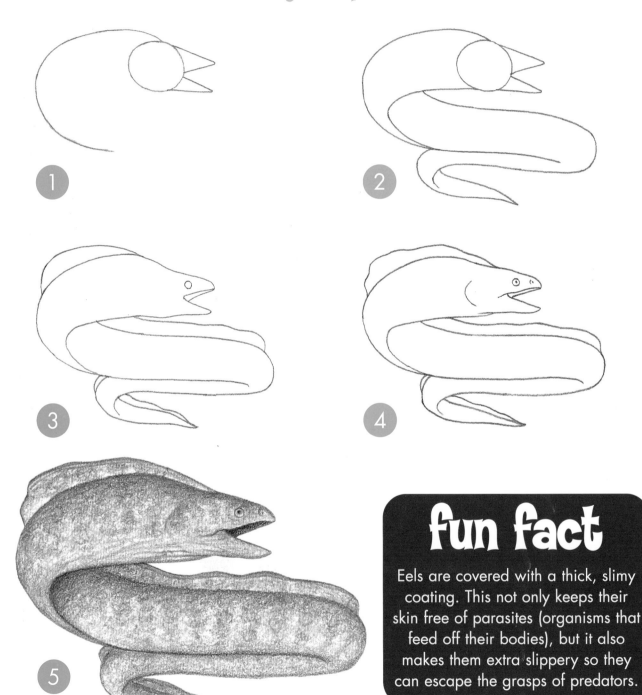

fun fact

Eels are covered with a thick, slimy coating. This not only keeps their skin free of parasites (organisms that feed off their bodies), but it also makes them extra slippery so they can escape the grasps of predators.

Sea Turtle

Begin drawing this **shelled** sea **creature** using a small circle for the head and an egg shape for the body.

Walrus

The walrus is known for its **big, blubbery** body and its huge tusks, which can be up to 3 feet long!

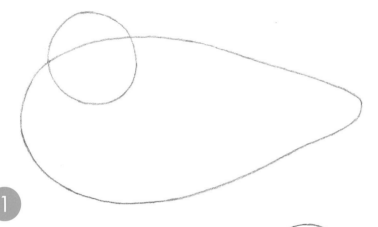

1

fun fact

Male walruses (also called "bulls") can weigh a whopping 3,700 pounds! As a result, they have to use their strong tusks to help pull themselves out of the water and onto the ice.

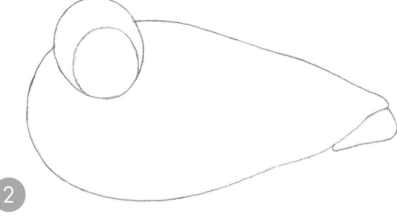

2

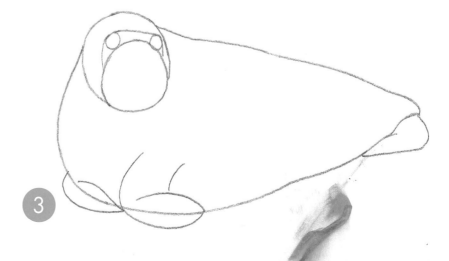

3

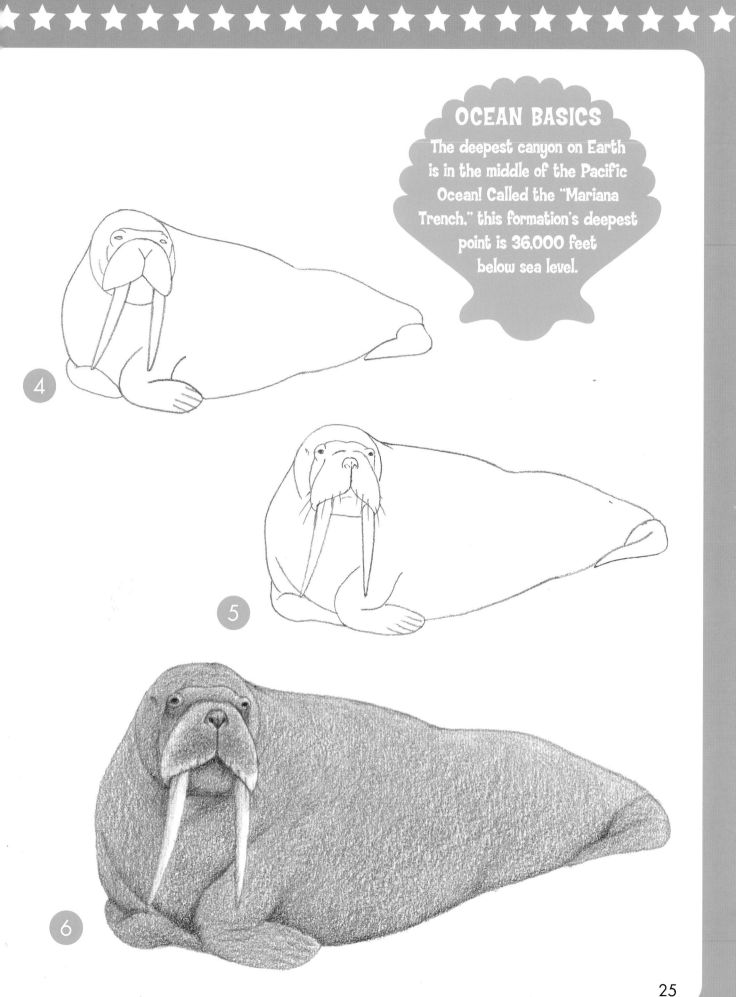

OCEAN BASICS
The deepest canyon on Earth is in the middle of the Pacific Ocean! Called the "Mariana Trench," this formation's deepest point is 36,000 feet below sea level.

4

5

6

Jellyfish

A jellyfish looks like a **bell** with **ribbons** trailing behind it.
But don't be fooled by its beauty: The "ribbons" are tentacles that sting!

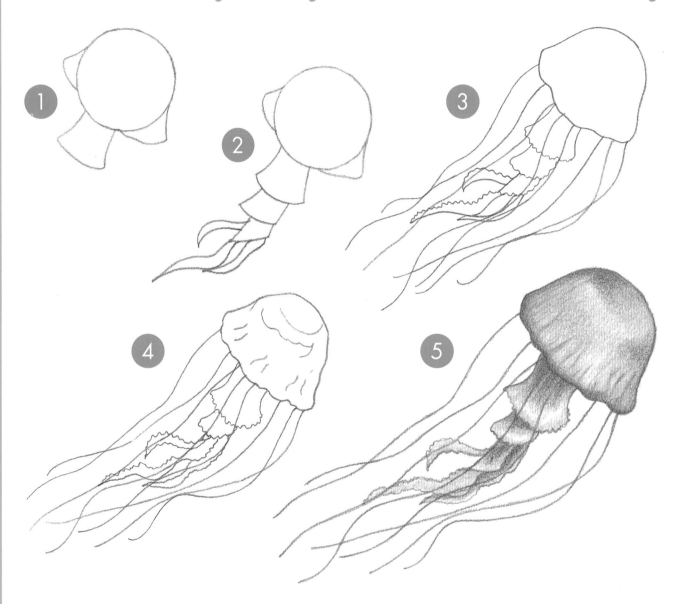

fun fact

Surprisingly the jellyfish has no lungs, gills, or any internal organs for breathing. Instead it "breathes" through the thin walls of its body and its long, stringy tentacles.

Swordfish

This fish's long, sharp **bill** resembles a **sword,** creating a streamlined shape that's perfect for speedy swimming!

Tiger Shark

Why is the tiger shark so **easy** to **pick out** in a lineup?
Because it has dark markings on its back that resemble a tiger's stripes!

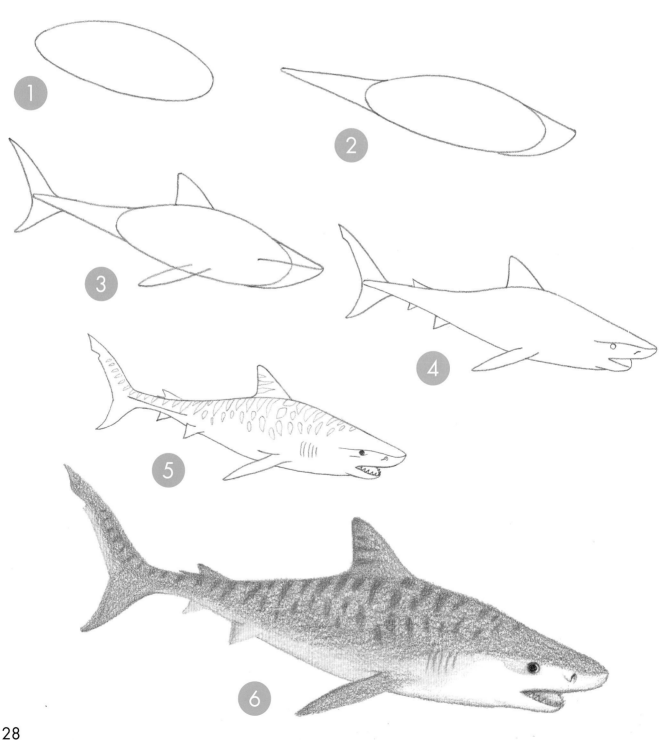

Lobster

This **crawling crustacean** is made up of many small parts: eight legs, two claws, six abdominal sections, two feelers, and one tail.

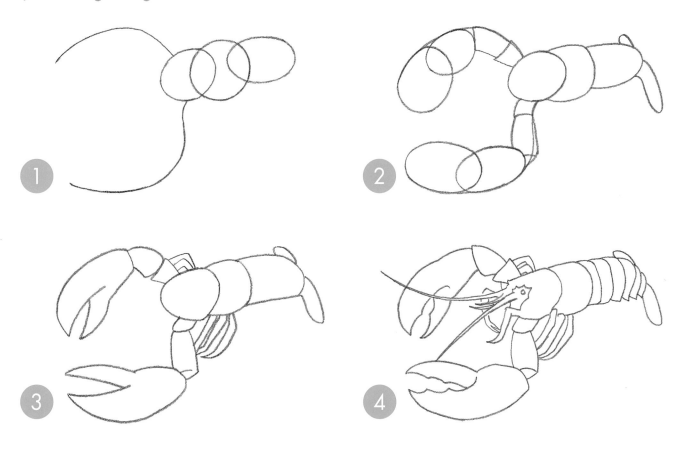

1

2

3

4

fun fact

About once a year, a lobster goes through a process called "molting." During this time, the lobster's shell (or *exoskeleton*) becomes too small and splits. The lobster then leaves its protective shell behind and gradually grows another one.

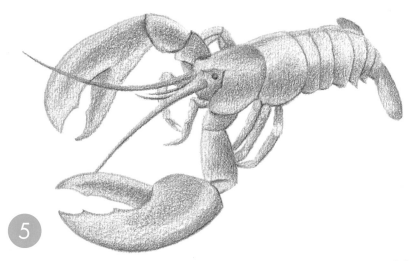

5

Sea Lion

Start this sea lion with a **circle** for the head and an **oval** for the body. Then finish with a velvety brown coat!

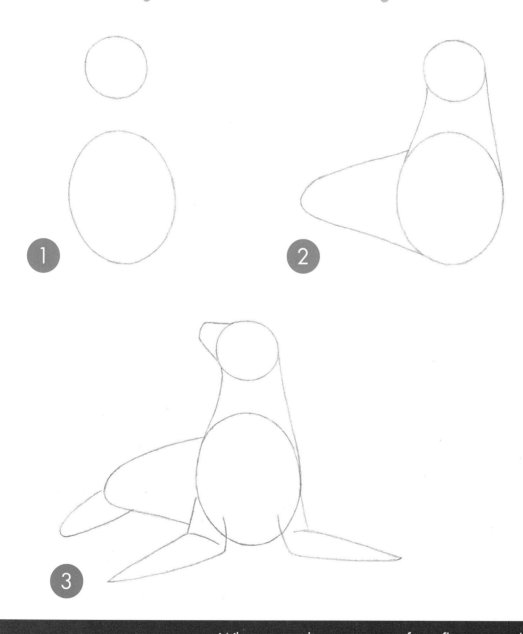

fun fact

When a sea lion swims, its front flippers push it forward while its back flippers steer. To help the sea lion move on land, the back flippers can also rotate forward under its body, acting as feet!

OCEAN BASICS

The average temperature of our oceans is about 39°F—only 7° above freezing! But water near thermal vents (openings that release heat from Earth's core) can be up to 400°F!

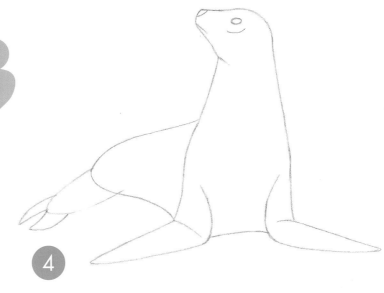

4

5

6

Porpoise

Although it's often **confused** with the **dolphin,** the porpoise has a less visible beak, its flippers are smaller, and it swims faster.

Sawfish

The sawfish is a **scary-looking** relative of the **shark.** But despite its long, sawlike snout, it isn't a danger to humans.

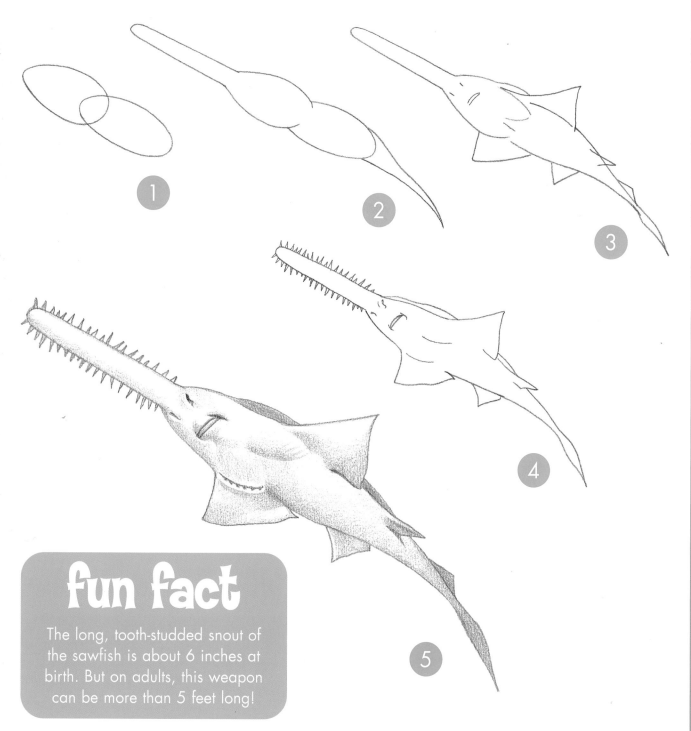

fun fact

The long, tooth-studded snout of the sawfish is about 6 inches at birth. But on adults, this weapon can be more than 5 feet long!

Orca

The **black** and **white** markings on an orca—
or "killer whale"—make this family-oriented animal easy to identify!

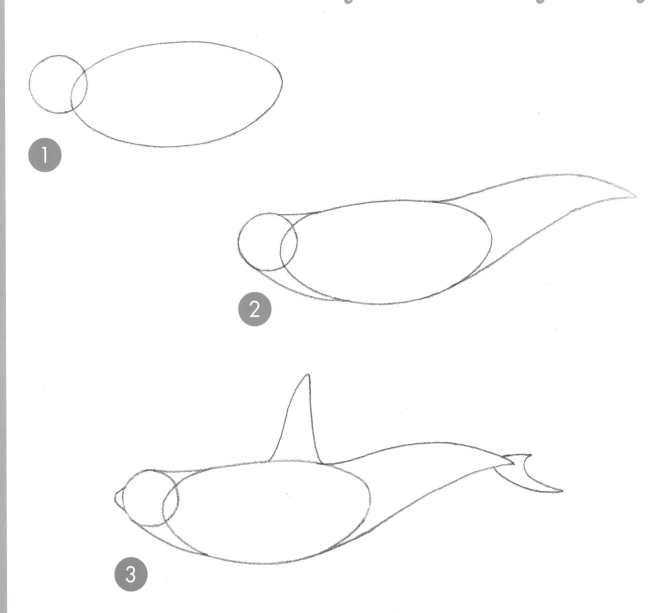

1

2

3

fun fact

The orca is an extremely skilled hunter, giving it the nickname "killer whale." But although it feeds on a wide range of prey—from small fish to blue whales— a wild orca has never been known to kill a human being.

35

Hammerhead Shark

This shark is named for its **flat, T-shaped** head, and its eyes and nostrils are located on opposite sides.

1

2

3

fun fact

Sharks have a sixth sense that humans don't: They can detect electrical fields around prey with organs called "ampullae," which help them find food in the dark ocean. Studies show that hammerheads have more ampullae than any other shark!

Octopus

The octopus has a **soft,** oval body and **eight** arms
covered with bubblelike suction cups.

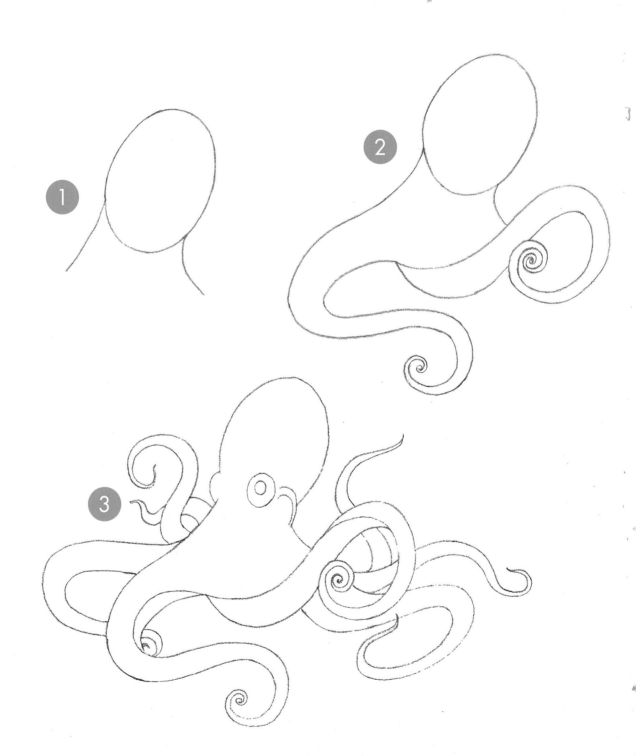

fun fact

This animal doesn't just have multiple arms—it has multiple hearts too! An octopus has three hearts: two for pumping blood through its gills to get oxygen, and one for pumping blood through its entire body.

Seahorse

This **critter** has a **horselike** head; a spiky, S-shaped body; and a long, curled tail.

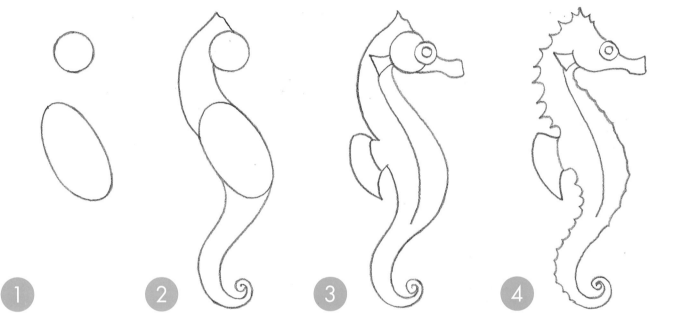

1 2 3 4

fun fact

Seahorses have a long, flexible tail that can curl around and grip nearby vegetation and coral. Because some seahorses are only 1-inch tall, they need their grasping tail to avoid getting swept away by the ocean current.

5 6